JAMES

BOOKS OF FAITH SERIES

Learner Session Guide

Mark Wickstrom

AUGSBURG FORTRESS

Minneapolis

JAMES
Learner Session Guide

Books of Faith Series
Book of Faith Adult Bible Studies

 Book of Faith is an initiative of the
Evangelical Lutheran Church in America
God's work. Our hands.

For more information about the Book of Faith initiative, go to www.bookoffaith.org.

Scripture quotations, unless otherwise marked, are from New Revised Standard Version Bible, copyright © 1989 Division of Christian Education of the National Council of Churches of Christ in the United States of America. Used by permission. All rights reserved.

References to *ELW* are from *Evangelical Lutheran Worship* (Augsburg Fortress, 2006).

Web site addresses are provided in this resource for your use. These listings do not represent an endorsement of the sites by Augsburg Fortress, nor do we vouch for their content for the life of this resource.

ISBN: 978-1-4514-0080-9

Writer: Mark Wickstrom
Cover and interior design: Spunk Design Machine, spkdm.com
Typesetting: Timothy W. Larson, Minneapolis, MN

The paper used in this publication meets the minimum requirements of American National Standard for Information Sciences—Permanence of Paper for Printed Library Materials, ANSI Z329.48-1984.

Manufactured in the U.S.A.
13 12 11 10 1 2 3 4 5 6 7 8 9 10

CONTENTS

James 1:1-18

Learner Session Guide

Focus Statement

The power of God for living daily life is revealed in the collection of sayings in the book of James.

Key Verse

If any of you is lacking in wisdom, ask God, who gives to all generously and ungrudgingly, and it will be given you. James 1:5

What Is Wisdom?

Focus Image

© Radius / SuperStock

Gather

Check-in

Take this time to connect or reconnect with the others in your group.

Pray

Gracious God, thank you for revealing wisdom to us in the Bible. Empower us with wisdom to live faithfully in our daily lives. In Jesus' name we pray. Amen.

Focus Activity

Write down as many wisdom quotes as you can in one minute. "An apple a day keeps the doctor away" would be an example. When you have completed your list, put a star by those sayings you have actually followed in your life. What do you observe?

Notes

Open Scripture

Read James 1:1-18.

- How did you feel as you heard this text read?

- What words or phrases stand out the most to you?

- What questions do you have about this text?

Join the Conversation

Literary Context

1. James is a letter that begins, like other letters in ancient times, by identifying the writer and recipient(s) and offering a salutation or greeting. The main theme of James and the key to understanding and appreciating this letter is wisdom. *Wisdom* here means the creative gift of God that enables God's people to live and grow in responsible maturity. This advice for responsible, faithful behavior is scattered throughout James like "pearls" of wisdom.

- Read James 1:1-4 and underline words and phrases indicating that James is a letter.
- Review James 1:1-18. Where does wisdom or the "word of truth" (1:18) come from, and how do we receive it?

2. Not only is wisdom the main theme and key to understanding and appreciating James, but also the letter is made up of a specific type of writing called *wisdom literature*. This type of writing has a rich tradition in the Old Testament and appears in many places in the New Testament as well, including Jesus' teachings in the Sermon on the Mount (Matthew 5–7). Wisdom literature communicates advice and instructions from one in authority (a king, teacher, or parent), based

Notes

on his or her experience of how to lead a successful life. In wisdom literature, wisdom is God's perfect gift. It belongs to God's goodness and purpose in creation, and it empowers all of creation, especially those who know the fear of the Lord (respecting and honoring God, living according to God's commands) as the beginning of wisdom. As you read through wisdom literature, wisdom sometimes speaks as "I" (in Proverbs 1:23-26, for example).

• What evidence do you find in James 1:1-18 that it is part of the wisdom literature in the Bible?

• Read Proverbs 1:1-9 and 20-33; Proverbs 9:10; and Psalm 111:10. List the benefits that are in store for the person who heeds wisdom.

• Read 1 Kings 3:5-14—Solomon's prayer for wisdom. How does this compare with James 1:5? King Solomon would have faced the temptations of wealth and power. Make a list of what James 1:12-16 says about temptation.

Historical Context

1. There is little detail in the letter of James to tell us who wrote it, when it was written, and who received it. Traditionally, the author is identified as James the brother of Jesus, who led the Jerusalem church until his martyrdom just prior to the Jewish war of 66–70 C.E. (Galatians 1:19, Acts 15:13-21). However, many believe that James was written by someone who dedicated this religious work to a hero of the faith, a common ancient practice. If this is the case, James may have been written as late as 130–140 C.E. The moral exhortation and references to testing, rich and poor in the assembly, doing business and making money, and laborers and harvest could fit with many times and settings. The address to "the twelve tribes in the Dispersion" is also unclear. It may refer to the early Christian community and its Jewish roots, or to the people of Israel in general— and so to all Christians also.

• What do you think about the fact that many things about the author, time, setting, and recipients of James are unclear? How does this affect the way you think about this letter?

2. Many writings and books were available to the early church. Early on, when Christians drew up lists of books that were accepted, disputed, and rejected, James was one of seven books that were disputed. By the fourth century C.E., however, the 27 books in the New Testament, including James and the other "disputed" books, became *canon*—or the standard list—for Christians in the Greek and Latin traditions. Since that time, many Christians have drawn strength, comfort, and power from the letter of James.

• How does this affect the way you think about James?

Notes

Lutheran Context

1. Martin Luther had questions about James. He believed that Jesus Christ, the cross, and the resurrection were at the heart of Scripture, but he did not see this reflected in James as clearly as in other New Testament books. Luther did include James in his translation of the Bible, however. He discussed it in prefaces to the New Testament and to the epistles and did not oppose people reading it. More importantly, Luther's theology, teaching, and approach to Scripture demonstrate his appreciation and use of wisdom.

- Read Luther's explanation to the First Article of the Apostles' Creed in the Small Catechism. What does God do? What does God provide? How does this compare with James 1:5, 17-18?

- Lutheran teaching emphasizes grace—the undeserved gifts of God poured out on us through Jesus Christ. Review James 1:1-18 and underline words and phrases that tell about God's grace. How are grace and wisdom connected to each other?

2. Luther taught that some books in the Bible, such as the letters of Paul and the Gospel of John, are more important than other books because they more clearly show who Christ is and what Christ came to do. This criteria or principle is called "what shows forth Christ."

- What do you think about the idea that some books in the Bible are more important than others?

- On your own, list the books in the Bible that are most important to you. Compare your list with others in your group, and discuss how you made your choices.

Devotional Context

1. Look again at the Focus Image for this session. You've probably heard of the phrase "pearls of wisdom." What pearls of wisdom have been important in your life? Did someone "give" you those pearls, or did you discover them on your own?

2. James 1:2 calls us to consider trials or times of testing as "nothing but joy." Tell about someone who faced a difficult time with joy. How was joy possible during this time?

3. James tells us to ask God for wisdom. We are to ask in faith, not doubt, which is "like a wave of the sea, driven and tossed by the wind" (1:6-8).

- Draw or describe how you would picture doubt, then do the same for faith. What similarities and differences do you see between doubt and faith?

Notes

- Write or say a prayer asking and expecting God to give you the gift of wisdom.

Wrap-up

Be ready to look back over the work the group has done during the session.

Pray

God of wisdom, thank you for showering us with every good gift. When we face difficult times, give us the courage to change the things we can change and to let go of things we cannot control. When we have doubts, be our anchor and strengthen our faith. Give us the gift of wisdom to live and grow in your grace. In Jesus' name we pray. Amen.

Extending the Conversation

Homework

1. Read the text for the next session: James 1:19—2:26.

2. Find three passages in James 1:1-18 that really speak to you. Write each one on an index card and carry the cards with you. After every meal, take out one of the cards and read it.

3. Check out the Book of Faith Web site at www.bookoffaith.org and consider starting or joining a conversation on the book of James.

4. Think about a trial or difficulty you are experiencing in your life right now. Pray for God's wisdom in this situation each day for the next week, expecting God to give generously.

5. As you review this week's session text or read the text for the next session, consider using the following questions to guide you:

- Which verse or verses causes me some concern?
- Which verse or thought enlightens me right now?
- Which verse or thought encourages me right now?

Be prepared to share your responses with the group, if you wish to volunteer.

Enrichment

1. Do some additional research on the meaning of *wisdom* in the Bible. For example, read about wisdom literature in a study Bible, look at an introduction to the book of Proverbs, or do an online search on the term "biblical wisdom." Prepare a brief report to share with the group.

Notes

2. If you are looking for insights on how to deal with trials related to addictions, check out a 12-step program such as Alcoholics Anonymous or Gamblers Anonymous. Check local listings for groups meeting near you. If you are looking for insights on how to deal with a loved one who has an addiction, check out Alanon or a treatment center near you.

3. Listen to a recording of the song "Turn, Turn, Turn (To Everything There Is a Season)" (Book of Ecclesiastes/Pete Seeger, Columbia Records, 1965) by The Byrds. The song is based on the wisdom literature in Ecclesiastes 3:1-8. What life experiences does it highlight? How many does it mention? They are presented in random fashion, probably because life can happen in just such random ways. Which of these experiences have you encountered in your life?

For Further Reading

First and Second Peter, James, and Jude by Pheme Perkins. Interpretation, a Bible Commentary for Teaching and Preaching (Louisville, Ky.: Westminster John Knox Press, 1995).

Available at www.augsburgfortress.org/store:

James, 1 Peter, 2 Peter, and Jude by John H. Elliott and R. A. Martin. Augsburg Commentary on the New Testament (Minneapolis: Augsburg Books, 1982).

Lutheran Study Bible (Minneapolis: Augsburg Fortress, 2009).

James 1:19—2:26

Focus Statement

God's gift of wisdom binds together hearing and doing, faith and actions, in Christian life.

Key Verse

But be doers of the word, and not merely hearers who deceive themselves.
James 1:22

Wisdom: Faith and Action

.·:·. Focus Image

In Christian life, faith and actions are joined together like inhaling and exhaling.
© Flirt / SuperStock

Gather

Check-in

Take this time to reconnect with the others in your group. Be ready to share new thoughts or insights about your last session.

Pray

Lord, thank you for the gift of wisdom that joins together faith and actions in our new life in Christ. Strengthen our faith and empower our actions for the sake of your kingdom. In Jesus' name we pray. Amen.

Focus Activity

Reflect on the Focus Image. Life is only sustained if we breathe in *and* breathe out. What do you think of the idea that faith and actions are like breathing? If you agree with this idea, which one is breathing in, and which one is breathing out? Why?

Notes

Open Scripture

Read James 1:19—2:26.

- What words in this text stand out to you?

- What feelings do you have as you hear this text read?

- What questions do you have?

Join the Conversation

Literary Context

1. James says, "Be quick to listen, slow to speak, slow to anger" (1:19). Compare this to James 2:15-17. How might we become more aware of the needs of others?

2. Throughout James, wisdom is the supreme mark of God's gift of creation. Faith is trusting in the power of that gift to help us weather the storms of life and grow to a maturity expressed in "religion that is pure"—caring for those who are poor and in need (1:5-15, 27). In this way, wisdom binds together faith and works, hearing and doing. This unity is as essential as that of body and spirit (2:26).

- Review James 2:14-26 on faith and works, one of the longest sections in this brief letter. List reasons why, according to James, it is crucial to see that hearing and doing, and faith and works, are bound together as parts of one action, like breathing.

Historical Context

1. Ancient Mediterranean society marginalized widows, orphans, and those who were poor, and they struggled for survival. Throughout the Bible, however, God shows concern for widows, orphans, and those who are poor, and believers are called to care for these groups.

Notes

- Review the session Scripture text and identify the passages that demonstrate this biblical concern for widows, orphans, and those who are poor, and the call to care for them.

2. In the Middle Ages, those in monasteries were obligated to help anyone who asked for food or shelter. Some of the earliest hospitals in Europe and America were established by Christians. Still today, many hospitals, long-term care facilities, and organizations that assist with other needs have a Christian background or mission.

- Based on James 1:19—2:26, how would you explain this care and concern for people in need?

Lutheran Context

1. In Martin Luther's time, the church emphasized works or actions as the way to earn salvation. In contrast to this, Luther's insight on justification by grace through faith put the focus on what God has already accomplished, rather than on what we do. Salvation, Luther said, is not something we earn by what we do. It is a gracious gift of God that comes to us through the suffering, death, and resurrection of Jesus Christ.

- Review the session Scripture text and identify why it is important to have faith and works together. Discuss whether James contradicts what Luther says about how we are saved.

2. In Baptism we are given new life, which sets us free to be what God intended all along. We are called to love and care for the neighbor. Luther referred to this baptismal calling as our *vocation*. We can carry out our vocation to serve others in many ways—as employers, employees, parents, siblings, children, friends, neighbors, and so on.

- List the ways you currently carry out your vocation. Choose one item from your list and tell how you serve others in that vocational role.

- In our vocations, as in faith, hearing and doing come together. Give an example of how hearing and doing are essential to one of the ways you carry out your vocation.

Devotional Context

1. In the first century, common belief and practice dictated that the more powerful a person was considered, the better the seats he or she should be given at a meal or in worship. The practice of favoritism is condemned in James 2:1-11. James suggests that in God's kingdom, all people are of equal value and importance.

- Why do you suppose people who have power or wealth are often treated better than others? What prevents people from treating everyone the same?

Notes

• What forms of favoritism exist in your community, church, or workplace? Brainstorm a list of ways to deal with these forms of favoritism.

2. Consider these questions: How has faith affected what you do to serve and care for others? How has serving and caring for others affected your faith? Has faith ever strengthened your serving and caring? Has serving and caring ever strengthened your faith? Then draw or describe the relationship between faith and actions in your life.

Wrap-up

Be ready to look back over the work your group has done in this session.

Pray

Lord of all wisdom, thank you for saving us through your gracious actions and setting us free to follow your call to serve and care for others. Strengthen us to follow this call at home, work, and church, and with neighbors close by and far away. In Jesus' name we pray. Amen.

Extending the Conversation

Homework

1. Read the next session's Scripture text: James 3–4.

2. With one or two other people, or with your entire group, brainstorm a list of people you would like to assist in some way. These might be people in your congregation or people in need in the surrounding community. Choose an individual or group on your list and make arrangements to visit with them. Take some time to listen to the person or group to find out what forms of assistance would be needed and appreciated. You might decide to do a project once a week, once a month, or once a quarter.

3. Create a video that shows how not to treat visitors when they come to worship at your church. Have fun exaggerating what not to do. Consider when and where you might show this video to others in the congregation.

Enrichment

1. Watch a movie that captures the negative effects of favoritism, such as *Philadelphia* (Sony Pictures, 1993), *The Color Purple* (Amblin Entertainment, 1985), *Mississippi Burning* (MGM, 1988), or *A Time to Kill* (Regency Enterprises, 1996). Or choose a movie that captures the

power of treating people with equality, such as *Joshua* (Lions Gate, 2002), *Driving Miss Daisy* (The Zanuck Company, 1989), or *Remember the Titans* (Walt Disney Video, 2000).

2. During the week, journal about how your faith and actions are intertwined.

3. Write or say a prayer asking God for wisdom in living out your vocation to serve others.

For Further Reading

Fully Human, Fully Alive: A New Life through a New Vision by John Powell, S.J. (Argus Communication, 1976).

Reaching Out: The Three Movements of the Spiritual Life by Henri J. M. Nouwen (New York: Doubleday, 1975).

Notes

James 3–4

Learner Session Guide

Focus Statement

Wisdom's exhortations and commands represent the collective insights of the world. They are signs of God's sustaining care for the world.

Key Verse

The wisdom from above is first pure, then peaceable, gentle, willing to yield, full of mercy and good fruits, without a trace of partiality or hypocrisy. James 3:17

Wisdom: God's Sustaining Care for the World

⋯ Focus Image

© Martin Heitner / SuperStock

Gather

Check-in

Take this time to connect or reconnect with others in your group.

Pray

Loving God, we easily overlook the goodness of your law and the gift of your wisdom. Help us to see how your law promotes and sustains life, and how wisdom shows your sustaining care for all of creation. Be with us as we study and learn from your Word and from one another. Amen.

Focus Activity

Take a look at the Focus Image. How do you feel about road signs, speed limits, and other "rules of the road"? Where do you find "signs" of God's wisdom in the world?

Open Scripture

Read James 3–4.

- What words in this text stand out to you?

- How do you feel as you listen to this reading?

- What questions does this text raise for you?

 Notes

Join the Conversation

Literary Context

1. In its 108 verses, the book of James contains more than 50 examples of exhortations or commands. James sees these exhortations and commands in a positive way, as the collective insights of human wisdom. Given by God in creation, this wisdom is a major sign of God's grace (James 1:17-18).

Read the following texts and note how exhortations and commands are described as gifts from God that promote and sustain life.

- Deuteronomy 4:1-14
- Psalm 1
- Proverbs 1:1-7; 8:1-21
- Matthew 7:24-27
- Romans 13:8-10
- 1 Corinthians 10:23

Notes

2. Writers often use metaphors to illustrate a point or idea. Metaphors are images used to compare one thing to another. For example, in James 3:1-3, the writer uses the metaphor of a bridle and horse to illustrate how a small thing—like a person's tongue or speech—can have a large effect.

• Read James 3:1-12 and list other metaphors used by the writer. How do these images apply to the tongue, words, and speech?

Historical Context

Early Christians may have struggled to identify how the wisdom of this world (the sum total of all the commands and rules of the secular world) might be connected to the Christian witness to God's love and mercy as known in the life, death, and resurrection of Christ. In James, however, there is no conflict between the world's collective wisdom and God's grace. Instead, the wisdom of the world is simply one sign of God's love and care for the world. It is a gift of creation that God has bestowed on all people.

1. Describe how each of the following commands and rules sustains and promotes life.

• Look both ways before you cross the street.

• You shall not lie about your neighbor.

• Stop the car at a red light.

2. Brainstorm a list of additional commands and rules that sustain and promote life. How are these commands and rules gifts to us?

Lutheran Context

1. Martin Luther clearly saw that God's law and commands were connected to God's promises because they show the way in which God, through the resources of wisdom, preserves and sustains all aspects of life. Luther's major contribution to this discussion was his treatment of the Ten Commandments. Luther believed that the Ten Commandments were one of the most important places to gain insights into God's love and mercy in Scripture. He placed them first—in the position of highest importance—in his Catechism, which he saw as a summary of the whole teaching of the Bible.

• Read the Ten Commandments and the explanations of them in *Luther's Small Catechism* (Augsburg Fortress, 2008). Note how Luther begins each explanation with, "We are to fear and love God. . . ." Compare this with Proverbs 1:7.

• Choose one of the commandments and discuss how it shows God's love and mercy.

Notes

2. Luther talked about the place of wisdom, law, and commands in his teaching on two kingdoms. We live in these two kingdoms at the same time. In one kingdom, Luther said, God works, through the gospel of forgiveness and promise, to make sure that we understand that we are justified not by what we do, but through God's mercy and grace in the death and resurrection of Jesus Christ. Luther called this the kingdom on the right. In the kingdom on the left (the kingdom of this world or the world of creation), God works through law or commands to preserve and sustain life. God gives the resources of wisdom so that we can sort out or discern the best ways to preserve and care for the lives of our neighbors. This kingdom encompasses all the world's institutions and structures, rules and regulations. Here human insights and wisdom can develop and imagine better ways of living.

• Notice that God is at work in both kingdoms, in different ways. What are some other similarities or differences between the two kingdoms?

Devotional Context

1. "We are justified not by what we do, but through God's mercy and grace in the death and resurrection of Jesus Christ." What do you think about this statement?

2. Tell or write about something in this session or the Bible text that challenges or delights you.

Wrap-up

Be ready to look back over the work your group has done in this session.

Pray

God of all creation, you sustain and care for the world through wisdom and the law. Help us to appreciate these gifts and see you at work in the world. Empower us with your wisdom to care for the world we live in. Amen.

Extending the Conversation

Homework

1. Read the next session's Scripture text: James 5:7-20.

2. Make a list of rules and commands that you encounter during the next week. Which of these sustain and promote life?

3. Each day, choose one of the Ten Commandments and read through it and Luther's explanation in the Small Catechism.

Notes

Enrichment

1. View the movie *Luther* (Eikon Film, 2003) or at least the scenes of Luther being interrogated at the Diet of Worms.

2. Read selections from the book of Proverbs.

James 5:7-20

Focus Statement

Prayer, praise, confession, and healing inspire hope for a community as it waits in the promise of our Lord's return.

Key Verse

Therefore confess your sins to one another, and pray for one another, so that you may be healed. The prayer of the righteous is powerful and effective. James 5:16

Wisdom: Healthy Habits that Sustain Christian Hope

Focus Image

© Ikon Images / SuperStock

Gather

Check-in

Take this time to connect or reconnect with the others in your group.

Pray

Giver of all good gifts, you give us all we need for today and provide hope for tomorrow. Strengthen us to live in your grace as we wait for Christ's return. Amen.

Focus Activity

Reflect on the Focus Image. What do you think is going on in the illustration? What in life tries your patience? What is worth waiting for? Why?

Notes

Open Scripture

Read James 5:7-20.

- How do you feel as you listen to this text?

- What words or images stand out to you?

- Through this text, what is God calling you to do or to be?

Join the Conversation

Literary Context

1. People in the early church believed that Jesus would return to earth very soon. James says, "The coming of the Lord is near" (5:8).

- Read James 5:7-11 and discuss whether the return or second coming of Christ is reason for hope or despair, according to this text.

2. The whole focus of the letter of James and other wisdom writings is on resources for life in this world.

- Read James 5:13-20 and describe how each of these provides help for daily life: prayer, praise, confession, and healing.

- This letter begins and ends with wisdom and the power of prayer (James 1:5-8 and 5:13-20). What might this tell us about the writer? What might it tell us about wisdom and prayer?

Historical Context

1. The original readers of James were probably very familiar with the story of Job. At the beginning of this Old Testament story, Job loses his property, his children, and his health. Friends come to visit Job and offer explanations for the suffering he is enduring. These explanations provide no comfort to Job, however, and he cries out to God. God answers by reminding Job of the vast universe made by the creator.

Job responds, "I know that you can do all things, and that no purpose of yours can be thwarted. . . . I have uttered what I did not understand, things too wonderful for me, which I did not know" (Job 42:2-3). God restores Job's property and health and blesses Job and his wife with more children.

- Review James 5:7-20, especially verse 11. How does knowing something about Job's story help you read and understand this text?

2. The prophet Elijah was also probably very familiar to the original readers of this letter. King Ahab ruled Israel during Elijah's time. Ahab and his wife Jezebel worshiped other gods. Elijah brought the message from God that there would be a drought because of Ahab's sins.

- Read 1 Kings 17:1-7 and 18:41-46. Then review James 5:7-20, especially verses 13-18. How does the account about Elijah and the drought affect your understanding of this text?

Lutheran Context

1. Martin Luther is quoted as saying, "Tomorrow I plan to work, work, from early until late. In fact I have so much to do that I shall spend the first three hours in prayer." Discuss what you think Luther meant by this. Would the writer of James agree or disagree with Luther on this?

2. Luther taught that one of the most important activities of Christian congregations is the "mutual conversation and consolation of the brethren." We extend friendship and fellowship in Christ as we reach out and share our gifts with one another in the congregation and community. We share the gospel, speak words of forgiveness, pray, and ask for God's healing with and for one another. This is one of the ways God works through us to keep us and sustain us in God's grace and mercy.

- How does James support what Luther taught about mutual conversation and consolation?
- Give examples of how members of your congregation reach out and share their gifts with one another and in your community. How are you involved in this?

Devotional Context

1. As a group, share a time of worship using the prayers in the order for Individual Confession and Forgiveness (*ELW*, pp. 243–244). Read Psalm 103 together as part of this service.

2. James says that prayer, praise, confession, and healing are resources for living each day and inspiring hope in Christ. Tell about a time when one or more of these resources strengthened you and gave you hope for the future.

 Notes

Notes

Wrap-up

Be ready to look back over the work the group has done during the session.

Pray

Lord, thank you for the gifts of prayer, praise, confession, and healing, which empower us for day-to-day living and inspire us with hope. As we wait for your return, help us to be busy ministering to one another and the world. In your powerful name we pray. Amen.

Extending the Conversation

Homework

1. Read the entire letter of James in the next week.

2. Consider participating in another Book of Faith adult Bible study.

Enrichment

1. Read the book of Job.

2. View the Wikipedia article "Christian Eschatology" (http:// en.wikipedia.org/wiki/Christian_eschatology). Here you'll find descriptions of different positions on Jesus' return.

For Further Reading

The Wounded Healer: Ministry in Contemporary Society by Henri J. M. Nouwen (New York: Doubleday, 1995). Offers suggestions on how to minister to others out of our own woundedness.

When Bad Things Happen to Good People by Harold S. Kushner (New York: Anchor Books, 2004). Provides a Jewish perspective on suffering.

CPSIA information can be obtained
at www.ICGtesting.com
Printed in the USA
LVHW060405290821
696362LV00019B/117